THE CITY OF YORK
and the MINSTER

By Amy Oldfield

Photography by Fre

Remains of St. Mary's Abbey Church. St. Mary's was a wealthy Benedictine monastery before its dissolution in 1539

Eboracum, Roman York, which by the 3rd century A.D. was the capital of Lower Britain, grew out of a camp which Petillius Cerialis set up in the year 71 by two rivers, now the Ouse and the Foss.

In A.D. 306 Constantine was proclaimed Emperor of Western Rome, later to become Constantine the Great, Emperor of all Rome and the first to become a Christian.

Anglo-Saxon York, Eoforwic, was the capital of Northumbria and the first Minster was built for its king, Edwin. As Jorvik it was a Danish trading centre and many present-day names of streets still have their Danish suffix 'gate'. William I used force to subdue the unruly north – he built two castles at York by the Ouse.

In medieval times the great Gothic Minster, wealthy St. Mary's Abbey and other religious houses were built and around the city a strong defensive wall was constructed with four massive gateways to command the main roads. At that time York was commercially prosperous with gilds for every trade to protect members. In 1392 Richard II conferred upon the Chief Magistrate the title of *Lord* Mayor. York is still the second city in England and though other cities have their Lord Mayor only those of London and York may use the prefix 'the Right Honourable'.

Charles I had his headquarters at King's Manor in York in 1639 and 1642. In the 18th century, York was the Georgians' social capital of the north. They attended its Race Meetings, saw famous actors and actresses at

Stuart Arms above the entrance to the famous King's Manor

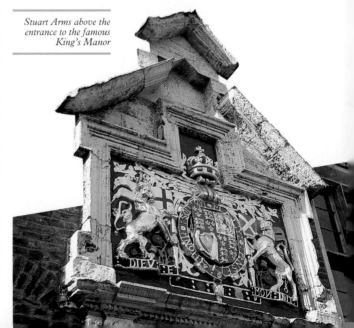

the THEATRE ROYAL (today still a leading provincial theatre) and danced in the ASSEMBLY ROOMS. Nearby, in Exhibition Square is the ART GALLERY. Roundels on the portico show notable York artists – Etty (painting), Flaxman (sculpture), Carr (architecture), Camidge (music).

William Etty, R.A., whose statue stands in front of the Gallery and facing Bootham Bar, was instrumental in preserving Bootham Bar when the Victorians would have removed it because of traffic problems.

The Gallery has fine collections of Old Masters, 19th and 20th century paintings, drawings and prints of old and modern York, stoneware, 18th century stained glass, porcelain and pottery.

In Victorian times George Hudson, a York citizen, helped to make the city the chief northern railway centre.

With the widening of streets and the establishment of modern shops some historic features have been lost, but the best will always be preserved as an integral part of England's history. For whilst industry and commerce are important to York's progress it is the historic past which gives the city its unique character.

The City Walls in Spring

Bootham Bar: one of the medieval city's main gateways

Coney Street: Viking Konigstrasse (King Street) which led to Earlsburgh, Earl Siward's palace

THE MANSION HOUSE in St. Helen's Square, the official residence of the Lord Mayor during his term of office, was built about the year 1725. The City's historic regalia and insignia are housed there, as well as a magnificent collection of civic plate.

THE GUILDHALL, reached through the archway at the side of the Mansion House, is a restoration of the 15th century Commonhall destroyed by fire in 1942 during an air raid and re-opened in 1960 by Queen Elizabeth the Queen Mother. The ancient stone walls, which escaped destruction, form the frame. The original oak pillars were made from single trunks of trees from the medieval Forest of Galtres and the pillars of the present hall from oaks grown on north country estates. THE WEST WINDOW tells the long story of York in five lights of 20th century stained glass, the work of the York glass-painter, Harry Harvey. On the wall to the right of the window is a bronze plaque which survived the 1942 fire. It was given to York in 1924 as an expression of friendship and good-will from the City of New York. To the left of the window is an wrought-iron balustrade given in 1960 by the people of Münster, York's twin city in Germany.

Adjoining the Guildhall is an inner chamber which survived the fire of 1942. It has panelled walls, two secret stairways and a ceiling

The Mansion House: residence of the Lord Mayor during his term of office

ornamented with old bosses. In this room £200,000 was counted before being paid by Parliament to the Scots for their help in capturing Charles I during the Civil Wars.

River Ouse with a view of the Guildhall in the background

West Window of the Guildhall

Printer's Red Devil looks down into Stonegate

Stonegate: site of the Roman road which led to the Headquarters of the Legions. Roman cobbling has been found below the present street level

Bible above a door of what was formerly a bookshop in Stonegate

Dick Turpin's Gravestone

ST. HELEN'S SQUARE was formerly the burial ground of St. Helen's Church, but after the Mansion House was built the gravestones were removed and the Square constructed. York was then the social capital of the north. At that time a journey to London took four days by coach, an uncomfortable and lengthy journey with the added hazard of attacks by highwaymen on the way. Northern families, therefore, preferred to come to York for 'the season'.

The notorious highwayman Dick Turpin was hanged at York in 1739. His grave is in St. George's churchyard, near Fishergate Postern. After he came north, Turpin – then known as John Palmer – was incarcerated in York's Debtors' Prison on a charge of horse stealing but later, identified as Turpin, was condemned to death.

York Minster

York Minster from the west

The Rose Window   *York Minster: Nave looking east*

YORK MINSTER is one of the world's famous cathedrals. A magnificent heritage from medieval days, its building between 1220 and 1472 has given it an amazing variety of architecture. The 13th century transepts have the plain lancets of the Early English style, the 13th/14th century nave and chapter house embody the grace of the Decorated Period, while the 14th/15th century choir and east end reveal the ordered beauty of perpendicular lines. Only the crypt is Norman.

The twin west towers, constructed between 1432 and 1480, are elaborately decorated and terminate in long slender pinnacles. In contrast, the central tower is plain, square and massive. The south-west tower houses the bells of the Beckwith peal and in the north-west tower hangs Big Peter, nearly eleven tons in weight and the deepest-toned bell in Europe. It can be heard every day at noon.

There has been a Christian church in this area since A.D. 627. Stone buildings followed the first little wooden church, both in Anglo-Saxon and Norman times, to be replaced eventually by the present Gothic cathedral.

The tomb of Archbishop Walter de Gray, under whom the building of the Gothic cathedral was begun, is in the south transept.

In 1968, during its restoration, a painting of the Archbishop in his robes was found at floor level on the coffin lid. Inside, together with his remains, were his chalice, paten, crozier and ring. These are now in the Foundations Museum.

Recent Restorations

In 1967 a colossal work of restoration was begun: 'tell-tales' had proved that the work was urgent. These are slivers of glass cemented over cracks; if the glass breaks it is a sure sign that there is movement, and within a short time after being positioned several did break, some at key points.

The first major operation was to save the central tower, which was in danger of collapse. Serious, too, was the plight of the east end – it was leaning outwards more than 60cm. The west towers also required attention and structural repairs to choir and Lady Chapel were badly needed. Soon, the interior of the Minster was a nightmare of deep holes, scaffolding and noise, while outside the loveliness of carved stone was defaced by a series of enormous steel shores. Out of crisis, however, came comfort in the knowledge that York Minster was universally loved, for with the launching of an appeal for £2,000,000, 80% of the contributions were raised in Yorkshire and the rest came from all parts of the world and from people of every race, creed and colour. Cleaning followed repair, the work being financed by a generous gift from the City of York and by other special donations. In addition, the 511 carved roof bosses were superbly decorated with gold leaf, an operation paid for almost wholly by the Friends of the Minster. Throughout the restoration years the Minster continued to be a 'living church', the daily services being held without interruption.

York Minster from the east

York Minster: Font cover in the crypt

York Minster: Chapels in the Crypt

The next major crisis came in July, 1984, when the roof and vault of the south transept were destroyed by fire. Most of the 68 carved bosses in the vault were lost and the famous Rose Window was saved only by the great skill of the Minster's glaziers. It has now been restored and replaced. The main theme of the new bosses is the Benedicite – O All Ye Works of the Lord Bless Ye the Lord – but among the smaller bosses are 6 designed by children as the result of a competition arranged by the B.B.C. television programme *Blue Peter*, on the theme of achievements of the 20th century. These include such subjects as *The Raising of the Mary Rose, A Man on the Moon* and the *Saving of the World's Whales*.

Minster

THE CHAPTER HOUSE was built in the 13th century primarily for meetings of the Dean and Chapter. An immense octagonal building with a conical roof, it is an architectural wonder in that it has no central supporting

Gold Chalice in the Foundations Museum

Blue Peter Boss (left): A Man on the Moon

Blue Peter Boss (right): The Raising of the Mary Rose

pillar, the downward and outward thrust of the roof being borne by the cross beams at its base and by massive exterior buttresses. 44 stone stalls have Purbeck marble shafts and canopies decorated with pendants of carved leaves and birds, and nearly 300 little stone heads which are beautiful, amusing, grotesque... according to the mood of the stone carver.

THE CRYPT supported the choir of Archbishop Roger Pont L'Evêque's Norman cathedral. Norman, too, is the Doomstone on the south wall representing Hell. The tomb of St. William, 12th century archbishop who was canonized in 1227, is in the western crypt. The Font is on the traditional site of the little wooden church – the first Minster, which was built for King Edwin of Northumbria after he was baptized at one of the city's wells in the year 627. Featured on the cover of the font are King Edwin and his Queen Ethelburga, St. Paulinus, St. Hilda of Whitby and James the Deacon.

THE UNDERCROFT – now known as the FOUNDATIONS MUSEUM – is beneath the transepts, central tower and parts of the nave and choir. Here one is able to walk among the foundations of former cathedrals, and, even further back in time, in the 4th century headquarters building of the Roman Legions. In the Treasury, priceless church and domestic silver is displayed including such treasures as the Horn of Ulf (given to the Minster in the time of King Canute) and a crusader's Heart Casket.

Minster Windows

The Minster is England's treasure house of stained glass; the collection extends over a period of 800 years. During the 1939-45 War 80 of the 128 windows were removed to safe places and their return was a colossal work of restoration which took over 20 years. The 3 largest are the Great East, the Five Sisters and the Great West windows.

THE GREAT EAST WINDOW, the largest area of early 15th century glass in the world, is the size of a tennis court. At the apex is God the Father with an open book on which are the words 'Ego Sum Alpha et Omega' (I am the Beginning and the End), setting the theme for the whole window.

To the right, attached to a pillar, are paintings of some of the Old Testament panels, with at its base tiny figures of the Dean and the Clerk of Works, who masterminded the 11 year restoration after the Second World War, and the glaziers who carried out the work.

THE FIVE SISTERS WINDOW in the North Transept is made up of 5 lancets each over 15m high and more than 1.5m wide and containing 100,000 pieces of grisaille glass. Charles Dickens in his novel 'Nicholas Nickleby' told how 5 York sisters were instrumental in its creation – alas, only fiction. Restored in 1924, it was releaded with lead which was found at Rievaulx Abbey and still stamped with Henry VIII's Seal, having been there since the Dissolution in 1539. The restoration was financed by the Women of England as a memorial to the Women of the British Empire who died during the 1914-18 War and whose names are recorded on panels nearby.

THE GREAT WEST WINDOW contains priceless 14th century glass with Biblical scenes and rows of Apostles and Archbishops. The magnificent curvilinear tracery is in the shape of a heart, often called the Heart of Yorkshire, which has recently been replaced by the Minster stonecarvers.

Other windows in the Nave include a fine Jesse and the popular PILGRIMAGE WINDOW with its monkey's funeral in the bottom border.

Great East Window

Great West Window

Five Sisters Window

Monkey's Funeral: Detail from Pilgrimage Window

THE ROSE WINDOW in the gable of the south transept is over 6.7m wide. Its main features are the 24 outer petals which display Lancastrian and Tudor roses between winding stems of golden leaves. The glass in the centre, added in the 18th century, is in the form of a sunflower from which golden rays radiate beyond a circle of blue. Golden suns in the outer triangular panels were added during the 1970 restoration, with the letter 'S' in each as a memorial to the Earl of Scarbrough, First High Steward of the Minster.

Walls and Bars

The Romans surrounded York with a timber palisading in the 1st century but replaced this with a stone wall. A fragment of the Roman wall still exists, visible from the street, in the grounds of No. 9 St. Leonard's Place. Beyond Monk Bar at the east corner, the Roman wall stands to a height of 4.8m. There are remains of the east corner tower, where the wall turns inward away from the medieval wall, having coincided with it from Bootham Bar to Monk Bar. It enclosed only 0.2km², whereas the area of the medieval city was over 1km². The Roman north-west gateway was at Bootham Bar, the south-east at King's Square and the north-east near Monk Bar. Part of a dedication stone found in King's Square and dating from A.D. 108 is preserved in the Yorkshire Museum. Substantial remains of the south corner tower lie at Roman level between Feasegate and Market Street. From there the wall went to St. Helen's Square (under which lie the remains of the Praetorian Gate, the main entrance into Eboracum) and on to link up with the Multangular Tower in the Museum Gardens. The inside of this tower may be seen in the grounds of the Public Library. Behind the Library, walls of various dates have been unearthed, as well as an ANGLIAN TOWER of the 7th century.

Micklegate Bar

Walmgate Bar with its Barbican

THE BARS, or medieval gateways, were built to command the main roads into the city. There were no side arches: these are modern. Every Bar had a portcullis (a stout criss-cross oak gate terminating in iron-shod spikes) and the added protection of a barbican (parallel walls built out at right-angles and terminating in a gateway).

Walking the Walls

THE MEDIEVAL WALLS, built in the 13th and 14th centuries, still surround the city almost completely, stretching for nearly 5km and offering the visitor a unique and interesting walk. (They are open until dusk, except in icy weather.) A good starting point is at BOOTHAM BAR, the gateway to the north. Here the wall went as far as the river, but was removed when St. Leonard's Place was opened out. The spikes of the portcullis are visible under the arch; the rest in the chamber above. To reach the walls ascend the stone steps at the side of the Bar. Between Bootham and Monk Bars there is a splendid view of the Minster. MONK BAR, which commands the road to the east coast, has a fine vaulted arch. Grotesque figures top the Bar, all holding stones. The doors out to the barbican are still intact and the portcullis can be seen from under the arch. Beyond Monk Bar, a length of Roman wall and remains of the east corner tower are visible from the medieval wall. The building behind them is the MERCHANT TAYLORS' HALL.

Descend at Peasholme Green. Here the damming of the Foss by William I produced the King's Fishpool of Fosse, making an effective defensive barrier. Even after the pool was drained, the land was too marshy to cross. Walk over the bridge and keeping the river on the right proceed to the RED TOWER, where the wall starts again. This is a 15th century brick tower, much restored. Walk to Walmgate Bar, which commands the road to the south-east Yorkshire coast. This Bar has the only complete town's barbican in England. The Elizabethan house on the Bar's inner face was originally occupied by the gate-keeper. There is still a portcullis and stout oak doors which used to be shut each night.

The walls lead on past ST. GEORGE'S BAR, a minor gateway, to FISHERGATE POSTERN, which stood actually on the bank of the Foss when the river was wider. Cross the Foss over Castle Mills Bridge. The curtain wall of the castle is seen from here. Cross the Ouse over Skeldergate Bridge to reach BAILE HILL, a

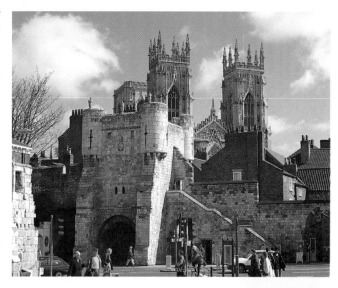

Bootham Bar

Plaque on Micklegate Bar

MICKLEGATE BAR

The Entry from London and the South. Here were exposed the heads of Lord Scrope of Masham 1415, Richard Duke of York (after battle of Wakefield 1460) so York may overlook the town of York - (Shak 3. Hy VI.1.4) The Earl of Devon after battle of Towton 1461 The Earl of Northumberland 1572 and many others, the last being the Jacobites Wm Connolly and James Mayne 1746. Date of erection 1196–1230 on older foundations; Interior renewed and beautified 1716. Barbican removed 1826. The Bar completely restored 1952

Monk Bar

grassy mound which is all that remains of William I's first York castle. Ascend the wall steps again at this point to proceed to Micklegate Bar. Victoria Bar in Nunnery Lane dates only from 1837, the year of Queen Victoria's accession.

MICKLEGATE BAR, which commands the road to the south, is the gateway by which the Kings and Queens of England entered the city. During the last 700 years most sovereigns visited their northern capital at some time during their reign. In 1971, the year of York's 1900th birthday, the Queen and the Duke of Edinburgh came that way in a great State procession, attended by the Household Cavalry, their approach heralded by trumpeters mounted on the Bar. Not so pleasant, the heads of traitors used to be exposed here, the last being those of two Jacobites, which were put up in 1746 – and only removed 7 years later when they were stolen! Micklegate Bar still has the doors which led out on to the barbican.

From here the walls lead on past the railway station to LENDAL BRIDGE, where the walk ends.

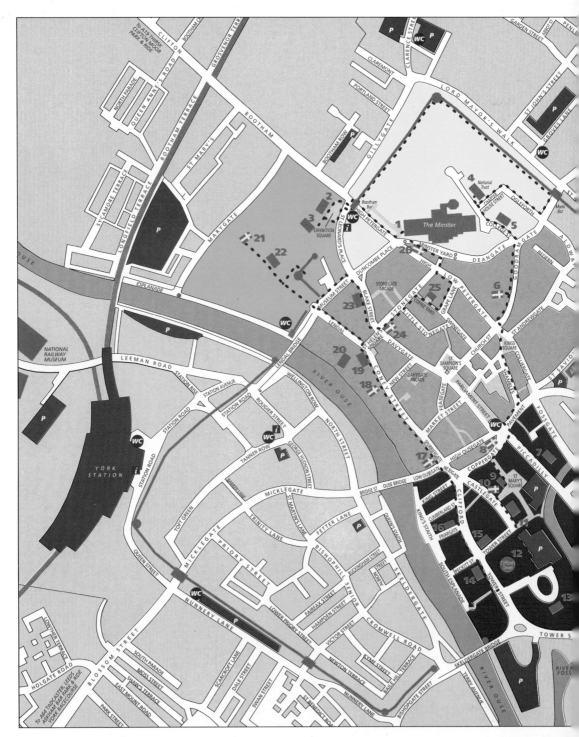

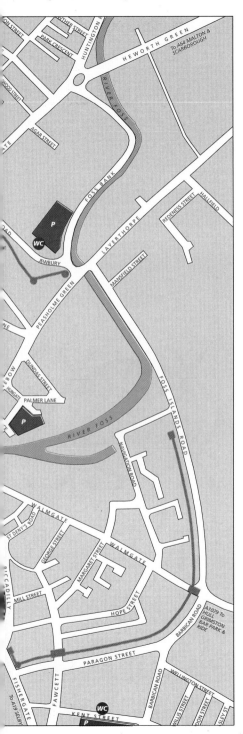

Allow at least 1½ hours.

(1) YORK MINSTER
Start from the West End and turn right along **Petergate.** Go through **Bootham Bar,** turn left and go up the steps onto the City Walls, opposite:

(2) ART GALLERY

(3) KING'S MANOR
Anyone who might have difficulty in negotiating the City Wall and its steps can turn right down **Gillygate** *after passing through* **Bootham Bar** *and then turn right into* **Lord Mayor's Walk,** *turning right again into* **Goodramgate** *to re-join the walk from* **Monk Bar.**
Walk along the City Walls and descend at **Monk Bar.** Go straight ahead along **Goodramgate** and take the second right into **Ogleforth** and along to its end.

(4) TREASURER'S HOUSE *(National Trust)* is at the end of **Chapter House Street.** Turn left for

(5) ST. WILLIAM'S COLLEGE.
Go under the gatehouse at the end of **College Street** and cross the road, bearing half right into **Goodramgate** and along to

(6) HOLY TRINITY CHURCH on your right, behind wrought-iron gates. Continue to the end of **Goodramgate** and turn left, crossing diagonally through **King's Square,** to enter **The Shambles** in the far corner. Walk down, turning right at the end and taking the first left at the traffic lights into **Piccadilly** to

(7) MERCHANT ADVENTURERS HALL on your left. Retrace your steps to arrive at

(8) ALL SAINTS CHURCH on your left at the traffic lights. Go sharp left into **Coppergate** and left again into **St. Mary's Square** for

(9) JORVIK VIKING CENTRE and, further round to your right

(10) ST. MARY'S CHURCH featuring the York Story. Turn left into **Castlegate** for

(11) FAIRFAX HOUSE. Then continue along to

(12) CLIFFORD'S TOWER and, just beyond it,

(13) YORK CASTLE MUSEUM. Walk around **Clifford's Tower,** entering Tower Street and passing the

(14) MUSEUM OF AUTOMATA to your left.

(15) THE REGIMENTAL MUSEUM is off to the right.

(16) FRIARGATE WAX MUSEUM is off to the left down **Friargate.** Carry on up **Clifford Street** into **Nessgate** and on into **Spurriergate** with

(17) ST. MICHAEL'S CHURCH *(now known as the Spurriergate Centre)* on the left. Walk on along **Coney Street** past

(18) ST. MARTIN-LE-GRAND Church on the left and into **St Helen's Square** for

(19) MANSION HOUSE and

(20) GUILDHALL.
Proceed down **Lendal,** past the main Post Office and cross the road into the **Museum Gardens,** site of

(21) ST. MARY'S ABBEY

(22) YORKSHIRE MUSEUM.
On leaving **Museum Gardens,** turn left and cross at the traffic lights into **Blake Street.**

(23) ASSEMBLY ROOMS are on the right. Re-enter **St. Helen's Square,** with

(24) ST. HELEN'S CHURCH just ahead of you. Turn left into **Stonegate.** Turn right into **Coffee Yard** snickelway to

(25) BARLEY HALL and on emerging go left up **Grape Lane.** Turn left into **Petergate.** Then take the first right down **Minster Gates** to find yourself opposite the South Transept of THE MINSTER, with

(26) ST. MICHAEL-LE-BELFREY on your left.

Suggested walk route

i *Tourist Information*

P *Car and Bus Parking*

wc *Public Conveniences*

Some Interesting Churches

St. Michael's Church (Spurriergate Centre)

Detail of one of the windows in St. Michael's Church, Spurriergate

HOLY TRINITY CHURCH, Goodramgate, was built in the 13th century and a chantry chapel added later. The glass in the east window dates from the 15th century and there is a Jacobean altar rail, box pews and part of a three-decker pulpit. The chantry chapel has a 'squint'. ST. MICHAEL-LE-BELFREY, opposite the Minster, is a fine Tudor church built as a simple rectangle. Its windows include good 16th century glass. There is an 18th century altar and altar rail. The 'Chrystenynges' Register of 1570 (now in the MINSTER LIBRARY) includes the baptism of 'Guy, sone of Edward Fawxe, 16th daie of Aprile'. The

Holy Trinity Church, Goodramgate

Roman Catholic Church of ST. WILFRID, Duncombe Place, has a fine carving over the porch of 'the Welcoming Christ'.

ST. OLAVE'S CHURCH, Marygate, reached through the Museum Gardens, was founded by the Danish Earl Siward and dedicated to the patron saint of Norway. It was largely rebuilt in the 18th century with stone from the ruins of St. Mary's Abbey. Its Norwegian flag was presented by the Dean and Chapter of Trondheim in 1939. There is old and modern stained glass. The tomb of Etty, the painter, is in the churchyard.

The slender medieval spire between Lendal and Ouse Bridges is that of ALL SAINTS' CHURCH, North Street, which is still furnished as a medieval church with several altars, shrines and a rood screen. Its stained glass is world-famous. HOLY TRINITY CHURCH, Micklegate, is all that remains of an Alien Benedictine Priory, which from the 11th to the 15th century was a cell of the Abbey of Marmoutier, near Tours, France. Ancient stocks are in the churchyard. ST. MARY, Bishophill Junior, off Micklegate, has Saxon windows and herringbone work in the tower. Inside the church is part of a Saxon cross; also a great round arch between tower and nave.

ST. MICHAEL'S CHURCH, Spurriergate, has a fine 18th century reredos and windows containing medieval glass. A redundant church opened as the Spurriergate Centre by the people of St. Michael-le-Belfrey, it still has a religious background.

ALL SAINTS' CHURCH, Pavement, has long been connected with the Municipal and Gild life of the city and the surviving gilds hold their annual services there. The 13th century doom knocker represents the mouth of Hell. There is a chained book on the carved lectern, 14th and 19th century glass, a 16th century brass plaque commemorating Sir Robert Askwith, Lord Mayor in 1609 and 1617 and a fine 17th century pulpit. The light in the octagonal tower, which once guided travellers to the city, now serves as a memorial to the citizens of York who fell in both World Wars.

ST. MARTIN-LE-GRAND, Coney Street. The former 15th century building was almost wholly destroyed by fire during an air raid in 1942. The south aisle was rebuilt as a shrine to citizens who died in both World Wars and in air raids on the city. The font cover, renovated after the fire, dates from 1717. Old stained glass includes the great St. Martin Window; modern stained glass in the east window was designed especially for the church. The clock which overhangs the pavement outside is topped by an 18th century naval figure taking an observation of the sun with an early-type sextant. The head at the side is of Father Time.

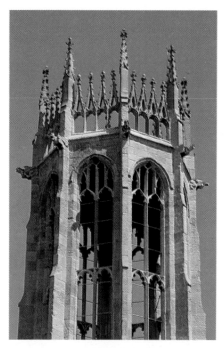

Lantern Tower – All Saints', Pavement

Doom Knocker: All Saints', Pavement

ST. HELEN'S CHURCH, St. Helen's Square, built in the 14th century, has several times suffered alteration. Interesting features include the 12th century font bowl, a carving of St. Michael and All Angels, a corbel showing a priest presenting a soul in a winding sheet to God the Father (unfortunately, the priest has lost his head). The east window contains good Victorian glass and the west window 15th century glass.

Two churches in Walmgate, ST. MARGARET and ST. DENYS, have interesting Norman porches and St. Denys has ancient stained glass. Roman stones are incorporated in the walls of ST. CUTHBERT'S CHURCH, Peasholme Green. General Wolfe's parents worshipped here before they moved to Kent; they lived in the timber-framed house opposite the church, now the Black Swan Inn.

ST. SAMPSON'S, in the centre of the city, is now a meeting place for pensioners. More than a thousand people visit it every day for rest, refreshment and companionship. Over the rattle of cups and saucers and the buzz of conversation, St. Sampson himself still keeps watch from the west window. At the same time it is still a living church with a celebration of Holy Communion every Wednesday at noon in a little chapel at the east end, site of the former sanctuary.

In CENTRAL CHAPEL (formerly Centenary), St. Saviourgate, there is a fine rostrum and organ case of Spanish mahogany. The chapel was opened in 1840 to commemorate 100

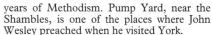

Holy Trinity Church, Goodramgate

years of Methodism. Pump Yard, near the Shambles, is one of the places where John Wesley preached when he visited York.

Stonegate and Petergate

In Roman York, STONEGATE was the main road, the *Via Pretoria*, leading to the headquarters of the Roman army which stood on the site of the present Minster and the land adjacent to it. Today, the earliest *visible* history in the street is Norman – the scanty remains of a dwelling-house which is reached through a narrow alley at No. 52A. For the most part, timber-framed buildings with over-hanging gables and the more dignified Georgian façades rub shoulders amicably with shops reconstructed in more modern style. High above the street is one of the few 'over the road' inn signs still left in the country. Near the entrance to Coffee Yard a little red devil squats on the wall, reminder of the 'printer's devil', the little boy apprentice, for here a printer had his business. A few doors away, a Bible dated 1682 hangs beneath an ornate carved doorway. Books were sold 'At the Sign of the Bible' from 1682 to 1873, including the first edition of Laurence Sterne's *Tristram Shandy*.

Within sight of Stonegate, but actually at the corner of Petergate and Minster Gates, sits Minerva, Goddess of Wisdom, her couch head a pile of books, her companion a wise owl. She is here because Minster Gates was formerly Bookbinders' Alley.

PETERGATE was the 'Main Street' *(via principalis)* in Roman York, extending from the *porta principalis dextra* (on the site of Bootham Bar) to the *porta principalis sinistra* (on the site of King's Square). Near the junction with Goodramgate a little tobacco boy, former trade sign of the tobacconist, stands above a shop. His kilt and tiara represent tobacco leaves.

The Shambles, formerly the butchers' street

The Fleece Inn pub sign in Pavement

Minerva, Goddess of Wisdom in High Petergate

York's longest street name for the shortest street

The Shambles

The Shambles is the oldest (and narrowest) street in York. It was mentioned in the Domesday Book and among the stallholders then was Robert, Count of Mortain, William the Conqueror's half-brother.

Formerly it was the Flesshamels – the butchers' street – the hamel being a bench outside each shop where meat was displayed. By law nothing could be placed under the bench, the space being left so that children could take refuge there from passing traffic.

There are only two Butchers' Gilds (original spelling) still in existence: London and York. The York Worshipful Company of Butchers had their Guildhall in the Shambles and at their Annual Feast the Master of the London Company is always an honoured guest, the main course being, naturally, a baron of beef.

WHIP·MA·WHOP·MA·GATE

The River Ouse

At York the Ouse is joined by the river Foss. Roman galleys and Viking ships came to York by water; Tostig and Harald of Norway sailed up the Ouse – to their eventual destruction at the Battle of Stamford Bridge; the stone for the Minster was landed at the Guildhall watergate; the Merchant Adventurers sent their cargoes of wool to Europe by way of the Foss and the Ouse. Barges still carry cargoes up and down the rivers, but the Ouse is now mainly a pleasure river with riverside walks, fishing from the banks, regattas, rowing boats and launches.

Three Bridges

OUSE BRIDGE was built about the year 1810. The first bridge, a wooden one, collapsed in 1154 and a stone bridge was constructed. That, too, collapsed, probably due to the weight of shops and tenements which lined both sides. A steeply humped-backed bridge was then built, to be replaced eventually by the present one.

LENDAL BRIDGE was built to provide direct access to the city's first railway station on Toft Green. It was opened in 1863 and was a toll bridge until 1894. Prior to the building of the bridge there was a ferry, the river being reached via the cobbled slope which still exists. When the ferryman lost his job he was given a horse and cart and £15 to help him earn a living.

Lights on Lendal Bridge

Lendal Bridge looking towards the Guildhall

View of Ouse Bridge through Skeldergate Bridge

SKELDERGATE BRIDGE dates from 1881. It has three spans over the water, one of which on the north east side could be raised to allow tall ships to pass through. Tolls were collected until 1914. A ferry had operated at this site for several centuries and at one period there was a ducking stool nearby.

Historic Buildings and Museums

Gray's Court, to the rear, was originally part of the Treasurer's House but is now the History Department of the University College of Ripon and York, St. John.

Nearby in Dean's Park is the MINSTER LIBRARY – the largest cathedral library in England. Among its 90,000 books and manuscripts are the priceless York Pre-Conquest Gospels which date from the year 1,000.

Regimental Museum, Tower Street

Two famous regiments, The 4/7th Royal Dragoon Guards and The Prince of Wales's Own Regiment of Yorkshire trace their ancestry back to 1685 when King James II raised regiments to assist him in dealing with a rebellion by the Duke of Monmouth. Both regiments recruit in Yorkshire and their battle

Clifford's Tower

CLIFFORD'S TOWER was the keep of York's medieval Castle. It was built in the 13th century, after the wooden Norman keep of William I's castle on this side of the River Ouse had been destroyed by fire in 1190 during anti-Jewish riots. It probably terminated in battlements, but the explosion of its powder magazine in 1684 destroyed the upper part. It is one of the very few quatre-foil shaped keeps still in existence.

Treasurer's House

TREASURER'S HOUSE has a secluded setting at the north-east corner of the Minster and its lovely garden provides an oasis of peace in the midst of the busy city. The residence of the Treasurers of York Minster from about 1100 until the Reformation, it then passed into private hands. It has been the home of a host of interesting personalities and many royal visitors have been entertained there. In its present form it dates largely from the 17th and 18th centuries, but evidence of the medieval house can be seen in the basement. In the cellars there is the base of one of the columns lining the Roman *Via Decumana* and it is said to be inhabited by the oldest ghosts in the country – a band of Roman soldiers.

By the 19th century the property had been divided into a number of dwellings and had fallen into decay. In 1897 it was purchased by Frank Green, a wealthy West Riding industrialist, who, with the help of the architect Temple Moore, recreated the now magnificent house with great taste and imagination. It has fine paintings, glass and ceramics, but is most notable for its collection of furniture. In 1930 Frank Green presented the House and its contents to the National Trust.

(Top left): Clifford's Tower

(Above): Treasurer's House

Inside the Treasurer's House

Regimental Museum, Tower Street

The Multangular Tower

honours emblazoned on their guidons and colours embody the history of the British army over 300 years.

The joint regimental museum at 3A Tower Street, York has the pageantry of the old regimental colours and guidons, the scarlet and gold of uniforms, the glint of weapons and the sparkle of medals to thrill the tourist and resident of York alike.

Museum Gardens

Within the heart of the city are around 0.4km² of botanical gardens, containing many rare species of trees, shrubs and flowers. Close to the east entrance are the remains of ST. LEONARD'S, a rich medieval hospital. Beyond on the right is the massive MULTANGULAR TOWER, west corner tower of Roman York, built about A.D. 300 and still Roman to a height of about 5m – the rest was added in the 13th century. Also in the gardens are the ruins of ST. MARY'S ABBEY church and the boundary wall with gatehouse and tower.

Yorkshire Museum

Set in the Museum Gardens is the YORKSHIRE MUSEUM, which includes an insight into daily life in Roman, Anglo-Saxon, Viking and Medieval times through a series of fascinating displays. Amidst the remains of the

Benedictine Abbey of St. Mary's are life-size statues of the prophets and reconstructed parts of the CHAPTER HOUSE with the great fireplace of the warming house in its original position.

On permanent display is the Middleham Jewel, an exceptionally fine 15th century pendant which was found near Middleham in North Yorkshire, home of the Neville family and Richard III, who married Anne Neville. This was purchased at a cost of £2,500,000 in August 1991.

A Roman soldier to be seen in the Yorkshire Museum

St. William's College

ST. WILLIAM'S COLLEGE is now the Minster's Visitor Centre, with 'The World of the Minster' featuring the life of the Cathedral over 800 years. There is also a centre for school visits, which serves as an introduction to the Minster for school parties, by means of audio-visual material, examples of stained glass, wood carving, stone etc.

Formerly, the College was the home of the Minster's Chantry Priests but at the time of the Reformation it became a private house. For around 6 months in 1642, prior to the

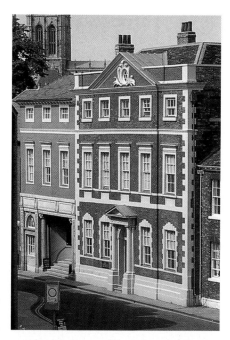

*Fairfax House,
Castlegate*

*Middleham Jewel.
Reproduced by courtesy
of the Yorkshire Museum*

outbreak of the Civil War, it housed the printing press of Charles I.

Above the outer doorway is the seated figure of St. William, 12th century Archbishop of York, and under the overhanging eaves are carved figures of the Virgin and Child at one

*Henry VIII and Anne
Boleyn, Friargate Wax
Museum*

St. William's College

side and St. Christopher at the other. The doors are modern and bear the mouse trade mark of Robert 'Mousey' Thompson of Kilburn.

Wax Museum

Situated near York's picturesque riverside and housed in a listed building, the former

city police station, the FRIARGATE MUSEUM is taking a leading rôle in bringing history alive, both for adult visitors and school parties. Among the many exhibits are life-size models of kings and queens, statesmen and famous personalities, from the days of King Alfred to the present Royal Family. They wear authentic costumes and are displayed against reconstructed sets and artefacts. Special lighting and sound effects give a realistic live atmosphere. Among local and international figures are Guy Fawkes, Dick Turpin, Franklin D. Roosevelt, Mahatma Gandhi, Neil Armstrong taking man's first step on the moon, as well as the Prime Minister, standing at the door of No. 10 Downing Street – an exact copy of the most famous front door in Britain.

Fairfax House, Castlegate

FAIRFAX HOUSE, built by John Carr in 1762 for Viscount Fairfax of Gilling, is considered a classic architectural masterpiece of its age.

Certainly one of the finest town-houses of its type in England, it was saved from near collapse by the York Civic Trust and restored during 1982/84.

Of all who lived in and fashioned this house, it was Charles Gregory, 9th and last Viscount Fairfax, whose influence was the greatest. It was for his daughter, Anne, his only surviving child, that he bought the house and completely re-modelled the interior.

(Left): Inside Fairfax House, Castlegate

(Above): Half Moon Court, Castle Museum

(Below): Cobbled Street, York Castle Museum

In addition to the superbly decorated plasterwork, wood and wrought iron, the house is now home to an outstanding collection of 18th century furniture and clocks, formed by the late Noel Terry.

Described by Christie's as one of the finest private collections of this century, it enhances and complements the house and helps to create a very special 'lived in' feeling.

Castle Museum

THE CASTLE MUSEUM, the most famous folk museum in England, owes its inception to Dr. Kirk, a country doctor and an antiquarian who collected an immense range of objects that were fast becoming out-of-date. In the former Female Prison are included reconstructed streets, period galleries, little shops with their trade signs, a hansom cab, a coach house and coaching inn, and in the adjoining former Debtors' Prison the felons' cells have become memorial workshops to Yorkshire's dying crafts (engraving, clay pipe making, horn comb making, etc.). Only the condemned cell remains virtually unchanged. Reminders of prisoners still exist – leg-irons such as Dick Turpin would have had to wear; a rough Calvary carved on a cell wall; a verse on an outside wall. There is also an Edwardian Street, a pageant of English costume, old toys and games, a display of military history and outside, near the River Foss, an old corn mill.

The A.R.C.

THE ARCHAEOLOGICAL RESOURCE CENTRE in St. Saviourgate, run by the York Archaeological Trust, is a 'hands on' exploration of archaeology for people of all ages. Here one can talk to archaeologists, handle ancient objects which have been unearthed during archaeological

Barley Hall

Archaeological Resource Centre

digs in the city and play inter-active computer games. From time to time there are special exhibitions, activity mornings, lectures etc. The Centre is open all the year round.

Barley Hall

BARLEY HALL is the name that has been given to the house once rented from Nostell Priory in the 1480's by Alderman Snawsell, a former Lord Mayor of York and wealthy goldsmith.

As the centuries passed, building work concealed the house, until only the presence of a surviving medieval doorway in Coffee Yard – the passageway between Stonegate and Grape Lane – hinted at its existence.

York Archaeological Trust has painstakingly stripped away the outer layers and researched York's medieval achives in order to restore the rooms one by one to their former splendour, to recreate the original atmosphere.

A fascinating audio-tour is available to guide the visitor through the medieval rooms.

Merchant Adventurers' Hall

THE COMPANY OF THE MERCHANT ADVENTURERS was the wealthiest and most influential trade gild in medieval York and their 14th/15th century Hall is one of the most complete of those still in existence. The great hall has a fine open-timbered roof and above the 18th century rostrum (which came from the old Assize Courts at York Castle) is the Company's coat-of-arms which was granted in 1969 by the Garter King-at-Arms.

Merchant Adventurers' Coat-of-arms

Prior to that date they had used the Arms of the Merchant Adventurers' of England, which are over the entrance in Fossgate.

The Merchant Taylors' Hall

In Aldwark is the guildhall of the Company of the Merchant Taylors which received its Royal Charter in 1661, amalgamating the Taylors, Drapers and Hosiers together with the socio-religious Fraternity of St. John the Baptist.

Over the great fireplace are the Drapers' Arms and in the adjacent small Hall is a fine stained glass window by Henry Gyles, dated 1702.

Museum of Automata

An impressive collection of 19th century French automata, including musicians, clowns and acrobats, is contained within the

Museum of Automata

museum. Automata are mechanical figures and scenes that mimic the movement of living things and their long history is brought to life with the aid of the latest video, sound and lighting techniques.

Of especial interest to children is the Contemporary Gallery within the Museum, where visitors are able to crank handles and push buttons themselves to set the modern pieces in motion.

Merchant Adventurers' Hall

York Story

YORK STORY, in the redundant St. Mary's Church, Castlegate, forms an audio-visual introduction to old streets and buildings, so that in a subsequent walk the city and its long past may come alive, because so much has already been learned about its planning and development and the people who used to live and work in it.

There are tapestries, slide shows, tableaux and pictures, all of which portray different periods of the city's history; models which include buildings cut away to show the course of their construction; a small theatre where

York Story

(Left): One of the life size figures in the Jorvik Viking Centre

(Right): Coppergate Court and the Jorvik Viking Centre

pictures and commentary trace the uses to which the city's buildings are put by residents and tourists alike.

Amidst all the re-organisation, however, the church's history and architecture have been preserved. There is even a Danish dedication stone which proves the existence of a place of Christian worship when York was a Danish kingdom.

The Jorvik Viking Centre

COPPERGATE in the year 950 was one of the busiest streets of Viking Age York, or Jorvik as it was then called. Market stalls sold leather goods and jewellery, hens scuttled in and out of the low, dark, timber houses, the people wore brightly-coloured woollen clothes and from time to time played a kind of board game similar to nine men's morris.

All these details came from an astonishing archaeological excavation in Coppergate.

The best of the finds have been meticulously conserved and put back where they were found on Coppergate, as part of a completely new kind of display. Underneath modern York, visitors actually enter the Viking world, with all its noise, bustle, smells and colour, and experience just what life was like for the Vikings of Jorvik.

An introductory area places the Viking Age in its historical surroundings and answers some common questions. Then stepping into electric time-cars, visitors find themselves watching the present recede into the distance as events from history float by and they are carried into the past. At the end of this tunnel, they emerge on to the Viking street of